Michael ... l

PRAGMATICS OF ART

University of Canberra

Centre for Creative and Cultural Research

Series editor: Professor Jen Webb

ENCOUNTERS I

Pierre Bourdieu
in conversation with
Michael Grenfell

PRAGMATICS OF ART 4

University of Canberra
Centre for Creative and Cultural Research
Series editor: Professor Jen Webb

RECENT
WORK
PRESS

First published in 2019 by the Centre for Creative and Cultural Research, with Recent Work Press, Faculty of Arts and Design, University of Canberra, ACT 2601 Australia

ISBN: 978-0-64855-372-4 (paperback)

Publication editor: Jen Webb
Publication design and layout: Caren Florance
Cover: detail from IMG_1791, sourced from https://www.flickr.com/photos/helloturkeytoe/2716529565/ by Shane Strange

Series Introduction

The Centre for Creative and Cultural Research (CCCR) within the Faculty of Arts and Design at the University of Canberra focuses on applied research into creative practice. Staff, research students, adjuncts and visitors work on key challenges within the creative field and the cultural sector. The focus of our work is to conduct imaginative and practical experiments at the intersection of creative writing, cultural communities, and contemporary heritage practice. Many of the CCCR's members are creative practitioners who produce not only traditional scholarly outputs, but also creative publications and performances, exhibitions and exhibition design, and professional inputs to cultural and community institutions. Poetry, material poetics, narrative practices, play, and exhibition practices are at the heart of our research activity. In addition, the CCCR facilitates creative workshops with people suffering from trauma and related issues, and is developing knowledge and skills about the relationship between art practice, creative thinking, and resilience.

This series, The Pragmatics of Art, aims to model and disseminate the combination of practical and intellectual research that guides the work of our Centre, and to provide thoughtful contributions, from a wide variety of sources, to artistic and intellectual projects that both derive from and serve larger communities. The series represents a working laboratory for students, artists, and scholars interested in learning to integrate the arts and skills of artistic knowledges and design into other branches of practical and intellectual work in our society.

This publication, the translation of a conversation between Pierre Bourdieu and Michael Grenfell, sheds new light on Bourdieu's thinking, guided by the thoughtful questions and comments offered by Grenfell. Though I have been reading and applying Bourdieu since the mid-1990s, and deeply engaged with his methodology, in this conversation I find new insights, new clarities. Bourdieu is one of the most widely-cited scholars of the twentieth century, and continues to be discussed, debated, treated with deference, and/or dismissed.

For me, the great value of this conversation is that it moves past the exegetical, hagiographic or iconoclastic approaches to Bourdieu's oeuvre, instead illuminating his key terms and frameworks, providing information about how and why they were established, and how they can be put to work in the service of developing knowledge and understandings.

In the extensive Notes section that follows the conversation, Grenfell constructs Bourdieu's world, setting out a temporal, social and geographic map of Bourdieu's scholarship, the historical moment in which he worked, the points at which key elements coincide or divide, and the scholars working before or alongside him. Perhaps no one writing in English knows this material better than Grenfell, and I am delighted to see *Encounters I* emerge in print.

Distinguished Professor Jen Webb

Director,
Centre for Creative and Cultural Research
University of Canberra

General Editor,
The Pragmatics of Art

Foreword

Anyone who has attended one of my lectures on Bourdieu in recent times will have probably heard me recount the story of the first and the final time I met with him. The first was in 1981; *La distinction* had just been published, and he was in London giving a talk about it at the French Institute in Knightsbridge. At the post-talk cocktail gathering, he stood pretty much on his own in the corner while the other members of the party went about their social discourse; this was my opportunity to talk with him. Out of that came an invitation to visit him in Paris, and an academic journey that was to engage me for many years.

The final time I saw him was about a year or so before he died. Interestingly, it was again at the French Institute in London, this time at a symposium on intellectuals. When I had spoken with him a few days earlier in Paris, he said he did not know why he was going, and really had nothing to say. Of course, once there he had lots to say and was typically provocative with speakers such as Eric Hobsbawn over what they considered the 'obvious' differences between the UK and France. However, at the end of the symposium, it was as if one of The Beatles were in the room: he was surrounded by several lines of people, and impossible to approach anywhere near. All this reflects on the way the Bourdieu-phenomenon had grown over two intervening decades; and on a profile and status that seem undiminished now, more than fifteen years since his passing.

For myself, that initial meeting led to me being visiting scholar, three times, at Bourdieu's academic base in Paris—the *Centre de Sociologie Européenne*—where there was opportunity to quiz Bourdieu directly on his ideas and research projects, and an ongoing associate membership of the team around his main journal, *Actes de la Recherche en Sciences Sociales*. These were exciting years: in the 1980s, the romantic image of 'the Parisian Left Bank' still existed to a certain extent: there was a whiff of existentialism in the air, and we thought these ideas we were working with would change the world ...

It was also exciting for me personally, even if the gulf between French and British ways of thinking was so evidently enormous. In these early years I was able to turn it to my advantage, since much of Bourdieu's output was un-translated, and it was fun to attend conferences armed with Bourdieusian epistemology as potential critique. On occasion, and as my own academic career took various twists and turns—education, linguistics, art and cultural studies—I thought I had done with Bourdieu and was even keen to move on. However, invariably I found different areas of research literature lacking, which would lead me back to Bourdieu and his way of seeing a particular topic. His view always seemed to be so much richer and to have more potential than the versions coming out of academic traditions, which Bourdieu always referred to as 'Anglo-Saxon'. In many ways, I have written an embarrassing amount about Bourdieu and on using his approach, and he certainly has dominated my academic life. I state that with no apology, and even with a recognition that I still find his work canonic: open one of his books at any page and I am immediately drawn in to a fresh perspective that throws up new ways of seeing the issue at stake—a *metanoia*[i] indeed.

---

[i] Bourdieu uses the word *metanoia* to signify an entire 'new gaze' in the way we see the social world (see Bourdieu 1992a: 251). The word comes from ancient Greek and means literally 'changing one's mind'. However, it has other psychological, rhetorical and theological meanings involving the breaking down and rebuilding (even healing) of the mind—correction even—and repentance. Bourdieu's own literary training would have meant that he was aware of these dimensions of the word when employing it. Some have interpreted the word in terms of seeing the world through a Bourdieusian *lens*. Of course, the issue then is what exactly is such a *lens*, and it brings into focus individual interpretations of Bourdieu, which involve further issues of reflexivity and researcher objectification. Certainly, Bourdieu intended it as a revolutionary epistemological move involving instantiation of his theory of practice, and all that entails in terms of *breaks* (rupture, even, or refusal) from prevailing paradigms, and developing a reflexive relation to the social world— both empirically and research wise. See Grenfell (ed) 2014 (chapter 13), and Grenfell and Pahl 2019 (chapter 9).

In the course of my various visits, I undertook a series of taped interviews with Bourdieu, the recordings of which I have held onto over the intervening years. My intention now is to transcribe and translate them as a way of disseminating their content. The ones represented in this publication form part of a much larger text—about twice the size—which I did work on with Bourdieu, and he edited with me. The working title of this project is *Bourdieusian Meditations*, and the aim is twofold: first, to offer the texts with annotations that develop, explore and reference the themes covered more fully—this because there is often a lot in a few words with Bourdieu; and second, to place these alongside empirical studies where I have used the methods and perspectives in research practice. What is offered here in this present publication is an edited selection of the interviews. These are set out as they occurred, but I have heavily annotated the text with cross-references, comments and explanations to guide the reader towards further exploring the themes covered in more depth should they wish to do so.

Encounters II will be a fuller version of the same, with many more associated themes emerging, which will then be integrated with the empirical accounts. *Encounters I* might be seen as an Introduction, and here we find Bourdieu expressing himself simply, even in a mundane way. Yet I have found from experience that it is a simplicity that is rarely grasped in its complexity. As such, I hope reading the dialogues between him and myself will both offer preliminary guidance, and point in directions of deeper encounters, for those wishing to explore the meaning and potential of Bourdieu's work for themselves.

Professor Michael Grenfell
University of Southampton, UK

Encounters I

MG: So, I would like to begin by asking you about some biographical details first of all. Later, we can then discuss issues with respect to your theories. Firstly, can I ask you how you became a sociologist, how you chose sociology.[1] It was not the most obvious thing to do at the start, was it?[2]

PB: I did philosophy, I intended to do philosophy. I wanted to do research on the affective life. I began work on it, and then I went to Algeria as a soldier,[3] and I thought to myself—*en passant*—that I would do an ethnographic and sociological study on North Africa in order to get the French to understand the situation there, because I had the impression that the French understood it very badly. I wanted to do an 'activist' [militant *trans.*] book and, little by little, I got into it, and I continued for a very long time up to my return from Algeria. That would be around 1961/62.[4] I continued with my phenomenological research projects up to 1965/66, and then I did the studies on the sociology of education,[5] which somehow came from the same logical purpose that had pushed me to do the work on sociology of Algeria. I undertook to do research on students, and also to put a bit of clarity into the very confused debates about education at the time. At the same time, I continued to do what seemed to be very serious for me, which were my analyses on family

1

relations, on the Kabyle ritual, on the pre-capitalist economy, etc., and then, little by little, sociological work took on more importance, and so I went over to sociology; in some way, I ended my ethnographic work with the *Outline*.[6] Basically, I went from one choice to another without really recognising it ...

MG: So, it was more a practical than a theoretical need at the beginning?

PB: Yes, it was an 'activist' intention, to say something about the way things were. People used to say anything about Algeria. But I did not consider it important intellectual work.

MG: But, at the same time, you were interested in sociological theory as such?

PB: Not that much, really. That came later, little by little. With ethnology, I had various theoretical problems ... problems, for example, that I asked myself about Sartre[7]—I had also asked myself them in my phenomenological research. I took with me a whole body of work I had done on Husserl,[8] Sartre, Merleau-Ponty[9]—theories of emotions, of the affective life, about passive synthesis, or objective potentiality, about the Sartre/Merleau-Ponty debate, etc. I had problems with all these sorts of theories, and I obviously found them again in the empirical *field*. But, very quickly, these problems changed with structuralism,[10] with all the issues about theories of kinship.

MG: Were you not influenced by the so-called founding fathers of sociology—Émile Durkheim, Max Weber ...?[11]

PB: No, not a lot. Weber I read at the very beginning, when I was working on Algeria for my first small book, in order to understand the Mzab people who lived in the desert and who are Muslims but who, a bit like the Protestants, are puritans, imposing more discipline and asceticism on themselves than ordinary Muslims. I used Weber in order to interpret the characteristics of their world by analogy to the Protestant one, which I think, moreover, is true. But, mostly, I was working with *The Protestant Ethic* and some of the religious sociology.[12] As for Durkheim, for me it was terrible, from my time as a student. One might even say that collectively, as aspirant philosophers, we worked to become against everything that Durkheim represented.

MG: You mean the sociological tradition?

PB: Yes, there was a kind of horror of Durkheim. We did not want to hear him spoken about. He was despised, and I think that this tradition of contempt for Durkheim is still true for philosophers. I remember that when I came back from Algeria, I had an assistant's post at the Sorbonne.[13] Aron[14] said to me, 'You are a Normalian,[15] you are able to teach

Durkheim'. And for me, it was terrible, to have to teach Durkheim, nothing could be worst. I had read Durkheim as a student—*The Rules of Method*, etc.[16] Then I had to read them again in order to teach them, and it was then that I began to be interested because it helped me a lot with my empirical work on Algeria. Mauss even more.[17] Next, I went on to Weber, and I became very familiar with all those authors later. I taught Weber and I came across the notion of *field* which I had confusingly in mind while teaching it. I did not succeed in teaching the chapter 'Wirtschaft and Gesellschaft' about religious individuals.[18] That really irritated me; it was completely descriptive, a series of descriptive types with exceptions, and I did not see its sense. And then, one day, I began to draw out a scheme on the blackboard, and I said to myself, 'It is obvious, we have to study people in *relation*'.[19] And that became very easy. From then on, I was stuck with Weber's work ('the ideal prophet does this or that, etc.'), and I was practically obliged to paraphrase Weber then, based on the scheme—it was a kind of structural matrix. If I was able to do that, it is because at the same time, I was doing *structuralist* type research on kinship, on the Kabyle house.[20] I read a *pre-structuralist* text with a *structuralist* way of thinking, in such a way that I was able to say the most obvious things about it which, before, had not been evident at all.

MG: So, you thought of yourself more as an ethnographer than a sociologist?

PB: I think that is a false distinction that has no reason to be other than simply historical, which indeed itself is linked to the colonial situation. It has no other justification. I recently read a paper from an Indian ethnographer from Philadelphia. He shows how different places—Oceania, Africa—correlate with the type of specialist: theories of kinship, that is Africa; theories of power, that is Melanesia. He also shows that ethnographers do not know what to do with historical civilisations like India and the Arab countries because they are neither Western nor 'primitive'. There is really quite a large part, which is totally arbitrary in this division between ethnology and sociology. I do not think that this difference exists. Which is not to say that there is not really quite a lot to enquire about regarding differences between societies where *economic capital* is not concentrated, not more than *cultural capital*,[21] as I have written about in *The Logic of Practice* (1990a/1980). These differences, it is a science to integrate ethnology and sociology, which can explain them. Often the fact that they are separated results in very harmful scientific effects. For example, ethnographers often do wild sociology, even the best ones, while sociologists often do parlour ethnology. And, for myself, one of my best pieces of luck was to do ethnology before doing sociology. I think that it is a way of thinking that lives with me permanently now. For example, in my lectures at the *Collège de France*,[22] the Kabyles come back to me all the time—on subjects such as authority or nomination—and

I am able to talk about the problem of passing on names in Kabyle society. There are things that one sees much better in pre-capitalist societies; there are mechanisms that are much easier to see in these sorts of situations than in a masked form when they are hidden by bureaucracy: bureaucratisation often hides magic effects, such as nominations. In Kabylia, since there are struggles between brothers to take the name of the grandfather, we see very clearly that a name (or title) is an issue. When one ends up with bureaucratic systems and they say, 'I name you assistant professor at Southampton', we do not always realise that it is in fact an act of magic. Bureaucracy constantly undertakes magic acts; they seem rational and a part of our world. Moreover, it is even commonplace; we are used to them, so we do not see them. My work consists in putting together separate things, which nevertheless speak to each other. I have spent many hours studying the rite of circumcision, and then, in another direction, the scholastic rites. All this ends up with some quite extraordinary effects of *débanalisation*,[23] and once that begins to work, it works in two directions. I can see that the act by which I name you 'Brahim' is not the same thing as the act by which I name you 'President of the Republic'. It is very different: in one case, there is no guarantee from the state, it is not written down. That gives us both common anthropological foundations and principles of differentiation.

MG: And yet it is sometimes said in the UK that you are more theoretical than practical.

PB: It is because my work is not fully known.

MG: Even so, you do have a theory: this synthesis between objectivity and subjectivity—which is fully formed at the moment.[24]

PB: The most important part has not been published. I say that partly as a joke. But I do think that basically I have only published works from my youth. For example, in terms of the notion of *field*, people who have read all the articles will have an idea of what I want to do. I work on things for many years. I know at what point I have made progress in relation to what has been published, most notably in everything I do in my lectures in order to develop all these concepts—*capital, field, strategy*.[ii] We are a long way from the end.

MG: I wanted to ask you at what point the struggle between *subjectivity* and *objectivity* in France became evident to you. It is something that one comes across in sociology, but your work is the first I found where there is this 'synthesis', a practical

---

[ii]   My practice is to retain Bourdieu's key concepts in italics to remind us that they come with a special epistemological charge; i.e. that they should not be read in their everyday meaning/sense.

dialectic introduced. In England, there is a tendency to be one of the other—either subjectivist *or* objectivist.

PB: It is a debate that is so difficult that it never ends. If I could, I would show you a place in my book about Algeria, which actually is more a student's work, where there is already the notion of *symbolic capital*,[25] which I do believe is a central idea to my work.

MG: And what of the depth of such notions? Were you aware of their profundity at the time?

PB: At that level, no. But, for example, I remember saying that 'the tribe' is only a name, which exists symbolically, and I knew that it was important. But, all that was not really connected to the whole system of concepts as now. A fortiori, when you look at *Le déracinement* (1964a) or *Célibat et Condition Paysanne*,[26] in them, there is already, at that time, everything about objectivist and subjectivist problems—*habitus*. I am surprised when I re-read them that I did not make more mistakes: at the time, I was very confused, I struggled. It was very difficult.

MG: And when was that?

PB: That would be between 1960 and 1965. These were very difficult years. The idea that it was necessary to go beyond objectivism and subjectivism, I had that very early on, partly because it was the same thing that I was trying to do in phenomenology, for partly social reasons, which were connected to the fact that I felt the intellectualist side of things—of objectivism, which put people at a distance; but I also felt the utopian side—irresponsible—subjectivist. I had an intuition of all that. But I was not sure at all. And even today, I say to myself, 'But what does that mean?' For example, the notion of the *field* of power is immense progress. I had to go through all the articles, the studies, where people make enormous mistakes, even empirical ones, because they do not have this notion ... But at the same time, I do not ignore the difficulties that it brings up. The Anglo-Saxons generally have a positivist representation of empirical work: it is a social fact, it goes back to Bacon ... All that said, I think I am one of the most empirical of the specialists in social sciences. Simply, if people say, 'Bourdieu, it is theoretical', it is because they do not find the kind of empirical work that they are used to. I think there is a part of what we write in scientific articles that has no interest. It is done in order to conform to the rules of the profession. Very often, objections that have been raised in my direction in the United States come from people's prejudices: 'It is French—therefore it must be theoretical and not empirical'. Like we say, 'I am in Italy, therefore I get my wallet stolen'. In my case, this prejudice is totally unjust, because I have probably done more empirical work than most sociologists who we think of as empirical.

Simply, for me, things that we see as mistakes are really choices, and choices of the *construction of the research object*.[27] Let us take three-quarters of the Anglo-Saxons' work on intellectuals: they commit an absolutely massive error with their sample (a randomly selected population from a whole population). From a theoretical point of view, what is most important is the whole population. Samples—everyone knows how to do that; that is basic methodology. For example, for the sampling of professionals, what is the whole population? Am I going to put solicitors and lawyers together? In reality, there is a struggle concerning definition. For me, my first problem is to know how I am going to construct the sample. In order to do things that are theoretically correct, often I am obliged to do things which might be seen as empirically imperfect, because one cannot do better when we want to construct like that. For example, in order to do my work on the *Grandes Écoles*,[28] this empirical definition of science had imposed itself upon me: I had interiorised it, it frightened me ... I did an enormous survey, with thousands of questionnaires which I looked at, for which I prepared codes, etc. I waited almost ten years without daring to publish the survey; because, initially, the survey is not totally synchronic: it was spread out over several years, which leads to a problem of comparability (mostly for measure of cultural practice—'how many times have you been to the theatre since the beginning of the year?'). In some cases, I had a rate of response that went up to 80%; in others, it fell to 40%, etc., etc. You can do a survey according to totally different principles. For example, the Americans, who did surveys on the *Polytechnique*,[29] re-do all the same longitudinal studies, with the same statistics of the social origins of the students from its creation until modern times, with the same results. That has no sense, because in order to understand L'X, L'ENA,[30] for example, it is necessary to understand the totality of the space.

MG: I sense that sociologists have problems with speaking about 'space'. Symbols, values, etc. They are more secure with statistics.

PB: Symbols can give rise to statistics as well. You just have to find good indicators for them. For example, the Foreign Legion, decorations. In my work I code all that.

MG: Is it not difficult to quantify the value of a title, of someone's accent?

PB: I think it is one of the things I learnt with ethnology; what is more elusive than a system of mythical representations: warm, cold, dry, wet? You take the plan of a house, and what you have is a kind of objectified system, one that is completely unconscious. You take the daily schedules of people in the villages and you have the relationship between the sexes. One can always find ... simply,

I think that most sociologists have a very limited view of scientific rigour, because with a bit of scientific imagination one can always find indicators, even for things that are quite obscure and unreal. The things I am most proud of are my lists of indicators, as inherent to an academic world. Research work allows us sometimes to make hypotheses on important social realities, which are not very obvious, in quite an effective way.

Sociologists sometimes are attached to a sort of naïve realism: 'what I do not see, what I cannot touch, does not exist'. The idea of *field* as a set of invisible relations is one example perhaps. There again, in another sense, is the idea of *symbolic capital*: empiricists reduce this notion to one of prestige. What can anyone do with prestige? *Symbolic capital* is a form of power, which assumes knowledge, and which therefore exists in people's heads, provided they are structured in a certain way—that is structures of perception. We could develop the idea. If you then want to find subtle indicators of *symbolic capital*, indisputable, like this table, now the craft of the ethnographer is very important: ethnographers know how to look, take photos, etc. I took a couple of thousand photos in Algeria.[31] Most sociologists do not know how to look. They make up questionnaires and send out investigators.

MG: In England, when people talk about Bourdieu, they say, 'Oh, yes, the cultural capital man'. But, I think that social capital is perhaps even more important because we still have this sense of noblesse in England. In France, it seems rather to be a certain intellectual noblesse—for example, the status of the polytechnician, etc. For us in England, it is rather more one's accent, ancestors, etc., which still exists.

PB: In France too, this kind of noblesse still exists, but it has had to reconvert itself. Lots of 'nobles' accumulate academic noblesse and noblesse of birth. The ENA is one of the routes for these more or less ancient nobles, and adds academic consecration to other signs of noblesse—accent, presentation, etc.

MG: Yes, and qualification inflation is also very interesting. For your average person in England, an academic qualification is a way of going up in the world, but it is also very frustrating: there are social tensions as a result of the myths that still exist in the academic system, because there are not enough job opportunities for all the academic qualifications.

PB: It is similar here in France: there is a kind of collective letdown over academic qualifications. This is a phenomenon that one sees in almost all economically advanced countries—a kind of collective disenchantment on the part of a whole generation who believed in the academic myth and who have ended up seeing that they hold qualifications with little value.

MG: As a result of their *habitus*.[32] How did you come across the notion of *habitus* in the first place—it seems to truly be at the centre of your theory?

PB: Well, it is everywhere and nowhere. In my writing, I have again taken up the genealogy of the concepts of *habitus* and *field*. Aristotle spoke about habitus and that got taken up by scholars—so you come across it in Husserl, Hegel, Durkheim ... everywhere in fact. It really is quite a commonplace word in the philosophical tradition, about which people have said almost nothing other than 'dispositions' or 'way of being'. That said, all the people who have used it have drawn out a certain theoretical line, or orientation, even if it is rather vague and imprecise in the way they use it. For example, Hegel contrasts *ethos* with *ethic*, *Moralität* and *Sittlichkeit*, which is a kind of Kantian moral thing in which there are transcendent imperatives, irreducible to their realisation in practice; and then habits, as 'the moral' realised, which has become a permanent disposition. Dispositional concepts always appear with people who wish to express something about the unconscious, sustainable, linked to the body, but not conscious (as much in the subjectivist tradition—Descartes, Kant, Husserl— as in the intellectualist traditions of consciousness, of the subject as 'knowing consciousness'). When Mauss took on the notion of *habitus* it was in terms of bodily techniques. He said that, in 1918, when they wanted to get the English troops to march to French music, it did not 'work'—in this way of saying it—as the music was linked to a whole way of holding the body, a gait; and it is here that he uses the word *habitus*. People who use the notion of *habitus*, even if they use it weakly, really take on something in spite of everything. For myself, I needed to be able to give a name to something that was very important for me: that is, that the principle of practices is not a conscious subject, but something socially constituted, deeply corporeal, in fact a practical relationship with the world. The notion of *habitus* said that very well, as long as one knows how to give this very classical word its full meaning. It is the same situation with *field*, which is very much used in physics and linguistics, but people only get part of its meaning out of it.

MG: And market: that comes from economic theory?[33]

PB: It is more complicated than that. The market is an individual case of the *field*. It is the genius of Weber to have been able to transfer economic logic into the site of the economy of symbolic goods, in particular religion, which was a way of breaking from institutional naiveté, and also a way of formidable research object construction. What I was only able to understand little by little was that the application of Weberian metaphors from the economic economy to the economy of religion was only possible due to the fact that in the two cases there are *fields*, and the theory of *fields* allows us to establish and include all that, and to end up with an economic theory rethought as an individual case of a general theory of *fields*, with a quite different economic agent, quite different economic laws, with notions of supply and demand which are completely rethought. In other words, I do not situate myself in the logic of borrowing concepts from others. Obviously, when I can apprehend a concept which I have already come across, to my own way of thinking, I am not going to go without anything. But, basically, I have never proceeded like that—that should be clear from the way I have worked.

MG: We hear a lot about liberal economics, about the market. Is that why people are critical of you— because you seem to be borrowing notions from economic theory?

PB: Unfortunately, you know that one of the laws of scientific debate is that people give themselves permission to criticise things without asking themselves if they really understand them. For historic reasons, in the United States above all (as an imperial power, everything that is big must be American, everything that is American is big), even people who I like, who are of the left, who are against everything that is unbearable in their country, always say as an initial reflex, 'we have that; an American has already said that', etc. There is this annexation tendency. Often, people who do a lot of work, but have trouble understanding what I do, give themselves permission to say, 'but what the hell is that?' Perhaps in 50 years' time ... At the moment, it is all about what came from Vienna in the 1880s—they kneel down before it and cultivate it. There is a kind of snobbism among left-wing people: 'We need Vygotsky, Bakhtin, the Russian formalists', etc. One of the problems with what I do is that people, whether they are in the official establishment and have a rather fundamentalist view that 'Everything that is not formalised, is formalisable, does not exist', or whether they are in a more critical position, let's say Marxist—in both cases they are perturbed by my work. I think what I do challenges a lot of normal ways of thinking. And, then again, I am a victim of *fast reading*. When I see my books referenced, it is quite unbelievable, I do not recognise what they take from me, they get me to say almost anything. I think that is linked to various things: the whole tradition of fast reading, the imperial arbitrary (or even imperialist), the Anglo-Saxon academic system, with people with enormous teaching loads and who, in their lectures, run through functionalist theories along with structuralists and constructivist, in fact a whole mishmash en bloc. It is terrible. This culture of fast reading is a catastrophe because it kills slow thinking. For myself, I spent many, many months to read Weber line by line. And Husserl, let's not even speak about it. There is a kind of impregnation. I would never have been able to write 'Weber (1913)'; this way of doing references is quite terrible. When

I make a reference, I state what I understood, which is a way of offering it up for verification. That is why some of the criticisms that are made of me annoy me, because they have no basis in fact. 'So, he says "market", so that is marginalist, so he is of the right'. Or, 'He says "capital", so that is Marxist, and he is a Marxist'. Or, 'He talks of "norms", therefore he is a Durkheimian'. For the Marxists I am a Durkheimian; for the Durkheimians, I am a Weberian; for the Weberians, I am a Marxist.

MG: It is a struggle for classification.

PB: Exactly. No one says to themselves, 'But what if he was all those things at the same time?' And, if the reality of science was to build up instead of having ritual antagonisms, I think this is completely possible. It is very pretentious, but these figures like Marx, Weber and Durkheim thought about themselves with respect to each other, and we can succeed in seeing what each saw in the others, and therefore build up, synthesise, in a non-eclectic way. Often people only respect someone once they are dead. In order for them to read someone in the way they should be read, they have to be dead and buried, and then they have some cult status.

MG: When you speak about strategies, that they are neither calculated or conscious, I am a little surprised, as surely there is a whole hierarchy between what is conscious and what is unconscious.

PB: Well, I think a lot of strategies are automatic. For example, in the sports field, the fact of having to position oneself in a good place in order to receive the ball is a strategy, an orientated action in a complex sequence of actions and interactions, but which is not calculated as such, which is not at base conscious, a conscious position with an end goal. In fact, I think it is a bit artificial if you make an opposition between conscious and unconscious: in what is called unconscious, there is always some small part that is under control, a kind of vigilance. It would be necessary to do some sort of very subtle phenomenology of different relations to practice. With *strategy*, I have wanted to react against people who speak in terms of *rules*, Lévi-Strauss, etc. At the same time, I have not wanted that we take it as 'calculated, rational strategy'.[34]

MG: Speaking of these subtleties in terminology, when were you first interested in language *per se*?[35]

PB: Always, in fact. I began work on bilingualism in Algeria, at the time of the changes that I saw in language surveys. I made a lot of use of Weinrich (a link between Martinet and Saussure, and Labov[36]) who made space for social factors in linguistic contacts. That interested me a lot because it was a way to better understand cultural contacts, but I was not sufficiently capable in Arabic to be able to pursue the linguistic dimensions of my study. Then I did systematic observations in the Béarn—in the shops, in the street—I took note of the social characteristics of the speaker and the listener in order to try to see patterns. I was anticipating doing a statistical analysis. I had around 150 exchanges. One of the reasons that led me to write on language was partly in order to end the domination of the structuralists, and semiology, which was very powerful in the 1960s, and is alive and kicking in the United States today under the title of 'discourse analysis': it is more or less the same thing, but with a more rigorous methodology, as is always the case in Anglo-Saxon countries. They believe themselves to be very empirical because they record; and, because they have recorded two hours of conversation between a doctor and a nurse, they believe they have been in touch with the social structure. They are less pretentious than the French who are swollen with theory, but who do not escape a fundamental bias, which is to take discourse as A to Z, as sufficient in itself.

MG: In the very nature of language, you have spoken about 'antagonistic adjectives',[37] which exist, which are an expression of class struggle. Is that truly in the nature of language or simply that they are used as a way of expressing this class struggle?

PB: There are oppositions that we come across everywhere, and on which every social universe hangs its historical significations. In a society divided into classes, the opposition between high and low: there hang loaded social significations.

MG: You also speak about the expression of 'manliness' in language as a whole attitude to language. Is that also basically an issue of social class?

PB: Labov himself has shown that the relationship to language is very much rooted in the notion of virility, of masculinity. I have done two sessions of my lecture series at the *Collège de France* on *To the Lighthouse* by Virginia Woolf, where there is a quite extraordinary analysis of the relations between the sexes expressed through language.[38] Here, there are totally surprising things about social oppositions, which are, at the same time, biological oppositions socially constituted.

MG: If we can go back to the beginning of your career, can you say something about the creation of the *Centre de Sociologie Européenne*?

PB: Well, it is a little complicated. At the beginning, I had come back from Algeria—thanks to Raymond Aron (see Endnote 14), in fact, who got me back at the time when there was the threat of putsch by the army colonels (see Endnote 3). There was already a *European Centre for Sociology*, which had just been founded, and after a certain period of time, because it was not doing any empirical research, Aron asked me to take care of it. I got students to come in— Boltanski, Lagneau, Karady, etc. The Centre operated up until 1968 when it separated into two centres.

MG: And the *Actes de la Recherche en Sciences Sociales?*[39]

PB: That must have begun in 1975. People around me wanted it; although I was very hesitant about doing it. It is a terrible load. We began at a time of crisis, at a time when revues were disappearing, when large libraries were giving up subscribing to journals. Moreover our journal, such as it is, with all the illustrations, etc., demands a lot of work— and I am involved with everything: titles, typeface, selecting the texts, etc.

MG: And just before that, was 1968 a big influence?[40]

PB: Oh yes, our team participated in different ways—in some ways both sympathetic—we were completely for it—and at the same time rather distant. For myself, I went and spoke in all the faculties. But at the same time, I could see that it was rather ridiculous.

MG: You mean rather more a festival than a revolution?

PB: Yes, and not always a very pretty festival at that. It was often very belligerent, like the Chinese cultural revolution—young people wanting to argue. I said so a little in *Homo Academicus*[41] by quoting Flaubert:[42] the description that Flaubert gave to 1848 is applicable to 1968;[43] it was rather ridiculous and worrying at the same time—there were people in their 40s, somewhat failures, who took their revenge nastily.

MG: Is this book (*Homo Academicus*) an example of 'applied sociology', which you talk about in the interviews you did in Germany?[44]

PB: On applications of sociology, I was in Berlin, invited by a Trade Union—ÖKV—a transport union, who asked me to talk about the *Collège de France* report on education ... [45] It gave me a lot of pleasure to see that the text was being discussed in lots of countries; for example, an Italian union and the CFDT[46] decided to take the text as a basis for discussion between European unions. But going from analyses to proposals poses a lot of problems.

MG: Perhaps it is not the work of the sociologist to come up with proposals?

PB: Yes and no. What is important is to try and see how to give the maximum amount of force to a certain number of ideas. This implies compromise. If I do a text all on my own, it is considered scientific, and so has no social force. A collective text, signed by the whole of the *Collège de France*, must have a large symbolic authority—collectively. And in order to have this symbolic power, at the same time it is necessary to pay with a certain number of intellectual concessions. For myself, I wanted to see what we can do in order to give power to ideas. The report was not taken up by the government, who did nothing with it. But, that said, I think it is a text that works well. It is debated a lot.

MG: Sociology has perhaps become rather out of fashion. I think there was a real conflict in the 1970s between sociology and politics. To be a sociologist now is to be very criticised.

PB: I do not think that sociologists have a realistic view of their craft. The objective of this report is rather to give political and scientific respectability to sociology. In order to give power to the ideas that sociology has discovered, it is necessary to give respectability to sociology, and one of the forms of respectability is scientific respectability. And the fact that it is a report from the *Collège de France*, where there are all the most prestigious French scholars, that gives considerable force, since sociological knowledge is being ratified by the most advanced science we have. Very often, sociologists do not have a realistic political way of thinking. They speak all the time about scientific realism, quoting Marx, but that is something that scientific realism itself should teach: we are in possession of certain truths—do we want them to become active? In order for them to become active, what must we do? It is the same thing with the report on journalism:[47] how can we use newspapers without being used by them? It is a question that many intellectuals do not ask themselves. As a result they spend all their time playing up to the journalists. I am among those who believe that there is no intrinsic power in ideas, but one can make them powerful; that there is a real scientific work to do in order to make intellectual ideas powerful. We can well see, these days, that we are governed by people who do not have recourse to science in order to govern and, on the face of it, there is no inherent power in being critical. The issue is how to give collective power to intellectuals who are quite isolated.

MG: In your study of language and communication within a pedagogic context,[48] you speak about the levels of subjectivity and objectivity within the analysis, and a critique of the classroom language.

PB: The work that you are talking about is really quite old but attempts to go beyond the opposition between objectivism and subjectivism, etc., since we include objective analyses of comprehension, the extent of misunderstanding through language and, at the same time, the way in which teachers and students somehow negotiate their levels of communication. 'Negotiate' is not a very good word since it is more unconscious. How they come together—how they sort themselves out to act as if they are communicating when in fact they are not communicating—in relationships which are actually relations of domination and authority. Students are usually submissive, they look up to the teacher. That is part of the mystification. They say to themselves, 'If I do not understand, it is my fault'. They do not say, 'It is the teacher who uses an obscure language, etc'. For me it is an example of analysis. I did this work quite a long time ago—today, I would do it better. But it seems to me to be a very good example. For this text, I was very happy to see it come out, although it is a little old. It was done in the early 1960s and, at that time, everyone spoke about ethnomethodology.[49] And that amuses me these days when, in my sociology lectures in the United States, they set what I did up against *ethnomethodology*. This is a quite absurd opposition: in line with the type of work I have done, some can seem to be structuralist, while other works are constructivist. If you take *The State Nobility*,[50] for example; this is a book which is centred around, I think, enormous statistical analyses, and both ethnographic and phenomenological analysis about just what a dissertation is, as well as the way of writing, the categories of thinking of the professors, etc. There is in fact no ontological opposition. To take the two together is difficult. Even to write about them in the same book, I had a lot of problems. Most of the beginning is taken from a social constructivist point of view. The later parts are more around structure. It is very difficult to bring together.

MG: Looking to arrive at the ultimate revelation, there is almost an epistemological crisis these days in how researchers approach their work, which sometimes leads to a kind of hermetic nihilism.[51] The researcher sometimes becomes so reflexive that they are the centre of the research.

PB: And that this is enough. Yes, the famous 'linguistic turn'.[52] It is a catastrophe. As Thompson says, it is a kind of 'French flu'.[53] It comes from Derrida, Foucault, and the others,[54] and goes on by way of the Americans. All the French illnesses go over to the United States and they become worst there—and it's because these people (Foucault, Derrida) are philosophers and they have never really done any empirical work. And then, all this is taken up by people who do not always have the philosophical culture of the French, and they set it to work in a quite irresponsible way, which then ends up with an antiscientific nihilism which is very, very dangerous—very reactionary. For myself, reflexivity is supposed to improve instruments of knowledge, not destroy it.

MG: Well, it seems quite difficult to be both reflexive and objective at the same time. You write about the *objectification of the knowing subject*.[55] Would that be the way one needs to situate oneself as a researcher within the field? That seems quite difficult to do.

PB: That is true but, for me, it is easier than one might think. But there are always two things: to do the research, and to speak about the research. To do fieldwork is particularly difficult; and so people more and more talk about the difficulty of doing fieldwork and, little by little, that takes the place of the research. And all that in order to end up saying things that are really quite trivial, that one can go back and find in Malinowski.[56] I think it is a kind of rather decadent nihilistic aestheticism. I find it disastrous. I was, I think, one of the first, for example in ethnology, to insist on the danger of theory. It is one of the permanent themes in *Outline*:[57] the necessity to reflect on not only biases linked to the external, societal source, but also the biases linked to the status of the researcher, etc. [epistemological vigilance *trans*.]. It is one of the central themes—theoretical bias in writing and transcribing. I really insisted on all that: not at all in order to make ethnology impossible, but to be able to do it better; while, more and more, this kind of critique takes the place of actual scientific practice, and it is very often done by people who are not well educated theoretically, who do not really have the theoretical culture to do that. The advantage of being from a continental tradition is that a large part of the researchers have a theoretical culture which they acquired relatively early, of course with all the dangers that that implies, but it does give one a defence system. We are vaccinated, less naïve when faced with all that. I think that positivism, which is after all rampant in the Anglo-Saxon tradition, becomes quite fragile when faced with theoretical 'maladies'. I have seen quite shocking things: people who swing from scientism—really hard stuff—

to a kind of theoretical nihilism in the space of a lifetime. It is very surprising—the same people! I have seen wild quantitativists, who can only speak about regression analysis, etc., who suddenly start doing very bad philosophy.

MG: You have an article by Rorty there.[58] He speaks about a certain 'nostalgia' for an inner truth, a kind of epistemological nostalgia.

PB: I think it is so ...

MG: Well, you are a sociologist, but do you not think that the same issues and hypotheses are just as relevant across the social sciences?

PB: I do think it is the same for history, anthropology, economics. I think that the epistemological issues are the same—absolutely the same; simply, in some cases, for reasons which are connected to the nature of the object, which are connected to the tradition of the discipline, it is that anthropology seems to be ahead. For example, in terms of all the problems one can have with classification, anthropologists have been ahead of sociologists. Part of what I have done with respect to the theory of classes consists in bringing into sociology what has been gained in anthropology, as normally the two disciplines do not speak to each other. Therefore, I do think that the fundamental issues are the same, but they take on specific forms and, at the same time, the best in each discipline brings in things which another discipline does not have. Sometimes one just has to bring them all together. I think that this way of working, which is very costly and sometimes rather dangerous—because you do have to keep an eye on what you are doing—can become very powerful, and very effective.

MG: In terms of reflexivity, drawing on various sources, Husserl seems to have been very important for you.[59]

PB: Yes, I read him a lot when I was young. But then, that is what annoys me with ethnomethodologists … they know Husserl very badly. They claim to be following him all the time, but they only retain a small part of his work, which has been selected out by Schütz;[60] and then they have held on to only a part of Schütz as well. Therefore, in my view, from what they use they have lost the basics. French semiologists do the same thing with Saussure.

MG: Are we not talking about issues of *doxa* here—of orthodoxy?[61] Of doxa, which one finds in each of the disciplines in the social sciences, as a value base for what they do? That is why they tend to veer towards objectivism or subjectivism without being able to study the relationship between the two.

PB: I remember it very well: I was in a seminar a few years ago, and it was an illumination to be able to bring together Husserlian theories of *doxa*, of the doxic relationship to the world, with the analyses of the young Marx on *Practice*,[62] etc., and with everything surrounding thinking about theories of opinion and the like. These things had been separate for me. The fact of having been able to bring together these things, for me, was very important. I was able to think, with the same conceptual apparatus, things that were normally very separate.

MG: So, the practical act is both ideational and sensual?

PB: We have both in our heads: that is the opposition between theory and practice, thought and action. In fact, practice, when we speak about it, and we do speak about it very little in books, is described as a 'non-theory', 'non-*reflexion*',[63] etc., etc., while the idea in *Outline* at the outset was that there is in practice itself a logic and a *reflexion*. There is a way to reflect practically, which is not quite the discursive and meta-discursive reflexion that thinking uses. Thinkers think explicitly about things, which are already explicit; while in practice, there is a non-verbal *reflexion* which is immanent in the practice, and which is instantaneous—pure consciousness. So this idea that practice sets itself up as the non-reflexive to the reflexive is completely stupid. We could hardly go three metres down the road if we did not have a non-intentional intention, unconscious (consciousness), or even a non-reflexive reflexivity, as a principle of self-correction and self-control.

We might even say all that in a quasi-Husserlian language. Husserl was working on a rigorous description of the world as *structuring* and *structured*; *structuring* to the extent to which it produces anticipation, pre-perceptions, which organise the world for us; and at the same time *structured* because the principles of these pre-perceptions, of these anticipations, are themselves the product of experience in the world. He spoke about *habitualität*, which obviously is very close to the notion of *habitus*. Towards the end of his life he went from a philosophy of transcendental consciousness to a philosophy of practice (practice as consciousness and consciousness as practice), which is quite close to what I have been trying to express. But obviously, he did not have the idea that social structures can also be mental structures.

MG: That is how you give three levels for the analysis of a *field*: the *habitus* of those involved in the *field*; our position in that *field*; and the *field* in the totality of *fields*.

PB: Yes, there is the issue of the relationship between the *habitus* and the *field*: the *habitus*, which is constructed by the *field* and constructs the *field*. For example, you go to a university meeting ... you are in your *field*. Your *habitus* makes you perceive, for example, the hierarchies in a certain way. You do not see them in the same way as another who has a different *habitus*, developed in a different milieu;

and, at the same time, your *habitus* is part of what you have acquired within the *field*. So, there is a kind of dialectic between the *habitus* as being structured in the *field* and at the same time structuring the *field*, the perceiver, the organiser to a certain extent that is not simply mechanical.

MG: Can one see the same sort of dialectic in the formulation of academic texts: so, a text would be seen as both structured and structuring, and a writer uses their structured academic *habitus* to structure (structuring) it in their writing of text?

PB: The issue of the status of what one writes is complicated because, in fact, it seems to me that if one succeeded in doing everything that it is necessary to do—that is, to say, hold awareness of the position of whoever writes in the *field*—the effects of this position, awareness of the information used and everything to do with how it might be structured by the position of whoever produces it, etc. If one succeeded in doing all that, I do think that the product would be quite extraordinary—in fact, almost outside of the *field* in some ways. I do think that in order for science to be possible in social sciences, it is necessary to come up with things that are somehow 'torn' out of the *field* of production, and capable even of commanding their own reception. I think that that is not impossible. It is said that sociology is always condemned to relativism, since sociologists are part of society; it is the same with history. I think it is possible to succeed in saying some things about the *field* of which one is part which are independent of the effects exercised by the *field*, by undertaking a certain work, putting into place certain techniques, and reflexively monitoring their conditions of production ...

The scientific *habitus* can perhaps be autonomous in relation to the empirical *habitus*. For myself, when I am in a meeting, I am like everyone else: I am nervous, I am angry, like everyone else. When I analyse all that, I begin to operate a scientific *habitus*, which can objectify all that, which understands why the empirical Bourdieu was angry. Back in life, we once again become the empirical subject. But, it is possible to create a subject torn away from social forces ...

MG: ... in order to be scientific?

PB: It is possible through work, through collective monitoring.[64] Moreover, this subject is a collective subject, in fact; not an individual subject. The subject has more chances of being autonomous the more it is collective, which is to say that it draws more on what has been acquired and is available within the *field*—techniques, methods, concepts. The more the subject is collective and reflexive, the more they are separated from the empirical subject.

Endnotes

1   This question is not quite so facile as it may first seem. Bourdieu was trained in philosophy, and his first work in Algeria might best be seen as anthropological. Still, he adopted the word 'sociology' in the title of his first publication on Algeria, really to denote that he was providing a social taxonomy of the country. At the time, sociology was not highly reputed in France, and hardly taught in French education. Moreover, ethnology appears frequently as a point of reference in his work, and he was, later in his career (2000), awarded the Huxley medal for anthropology. All this to say, 'his' sociology—*la sociologie*—is very distinct from conventional forms, and might even best be understood as a kind of 'social philosophy' or 'philosophical anthropology'.

2   Bourdieu always insisted that his own biography was not to be detailed in interpreting his work and, for many years, remained cautious with respect to speaking about it in terms of his life and times. This line softened somewhat in later years, and for academic reasons of reflexivity, etc. See Bourdieu 2007/ 2004, *Sketch for a self-analysis*. However, even here, the book begins with the epigraph: 'This is not an autobiography'. See also the account of his final lecture at the *Collège de France*, which seems to suggest the work was 'all about me' (Eakin 2001). Also 'Pierre par Bourdieu—"Le Rosebud de Pierre Bourdieu"' (in *Le Nouvel Observateur* 2002). Although listed as such, this text was translated and published from German without Bourdieu's permission, along with testimonies from some who knew him at school and university. The whole amounted to an 'intellectual exposé' of sorts at the time, although the main text from him originated from the *Sketch* referenced above, which he was obviously preparing at the time. I attempt an 'intellectual biography', which

includes an account of his life, in Grenfell 2004, *Pierre Bourdieu: Agent provocateur*.

3   Algeria is a former French colony in North Africa on the Mediterranean coast. It was colonised by the French in 1830, and 'assimilated' into French territory. By the 1950s, however, it was engaged in a fierce war of independence, which also threatened to bring down the French state with its countervailing attitudes to Algeria. In 1961, a coup d'état was attempted by French Military Generals— *le putsch des Colonels*—who, opposed to the secret negotiations between the French government and the Algerian anti-colonial groups, planned to take over both key towns in Algeria and Paris, thus deposing President De Gaulle. Bourdieu was sent to Algeria in 1953, really to do his military service, but as a result was thrust into a combat zone, which involved numerous killings. See also Grenfell 2006, and Grenfell 2004 (chapter 2).

4   Bourdieu's principal publications on Algeria are: Bourdieu 1958; 1961; 1962a; 1962b; 1963; 1964a. See also Endnote 31 and Bourdieu (2012/ 2003) *Picturing Algeria*.

5   Bourdieu's seminal texts on education are Bourdieu (with Passeron) 1964b; 1977a/1970; 1979/1964. See also Grenfell 2004 (chapter 3); 2007; 2014c; and Grenfell et al. 2012.

6   Bourdieu 1977b/1972 *Outline of a theory of practice*. See also Grenfell and Lebaron (eds) 2014 Part 1; Grenfell (ed) 2014a (chapters 1 and 2).

7   Jean-Paul Sartre (1905–1980) was a French philosopher, novelist, biographer and playwright. He is known as being the principal founder of French existentialism, which is really immediately based around the ideas of Heidegger and Husserl (see Endnote 59), and previous existentialist writers such as Karl Jaspers (1983–1969) and Søren Kierkegaard (1813–1855). He is known particularly as a political activist; especially during the second world war

where men and women were called on to define their allegiances by their actions. Later he was a supporter of Marxism and the Soviet Union. His would be seen as the subjectivist side of the subject–object dichotomy.

8   Edmund Husserl (1859–1938) was a German philosopher who established the school of phenomenology: an approach, which focuses on 'things in themselves' as perceived/experienced by the 'structure of consciousness'. See Endnote 59.

9   Maurice Merleau-Ponty (1908–1961) was a French philosopher, who was an exponent of phenomenology as expounded by Husserl and Heidegger.

10 Structuralism is an approach in the social sciences that sees human culture in terms of relational structures—material and ideational. The leading exponent in France in the mid-twentieth century was Claude Lévi-Strauss (1908–2009). A later Marxist variant was also influential and proposed by Louis Althusser (1918–1990). These figures' works would be seen as the objectivist side of the subject–object dichotomy.

11 See Endnotes 12 and 16.

12 Max Weber (1864–1920) was a German sociologist. *The Protestant Ethic and the Spirit of Capitalism* was published in 1905 and translated into English in 1930. It is generally seen as a riposte to the thesis of Karl Marx, which stated that societal change—in particular capitalism—grew out of material conditions. In this book, Weber argues that a certain way of thinking—the Protestant work ethic—was a primary genome for material/economic change, thus suggesting an 'idealist' alternative to 'materialism'. This view was highly influential on Bourdieu and later saw him drawing on Erwin Panofsky to show how a certain way of thinking influenced material architecture. See Bourdieu 1971a/1967. See also Endnote 62.

13   La Sorbonne is one of Europe's oldest and most prestigious universities, founded around 1150 and based in Paris.

14   Raymond Aron (1905–1983) was a French philosopher, who also had a particular interest in sociology—really, at a time when it was not widely regarded, or even taught, in France. He was among the leading French intellectuals of his time; in particular, during the 1930s when they were seeking alternatives to traditional Catholic and economic/political thinking. See Loubet del Bayle 1969.

15   Bourdieu attended the *École Normale Supérieure* (ENS), one of the most prestigious of the *Grandes Écoles* that were formed by Napoleon in the nineteenth century in order to produce a highly educated elite for the country. The ENS is essentially a teacher training college, but at a very high level; all the famous French intellectuals attended it, including Sartre and De Beauvoir; Derrida was in Bourdieu's year.

16   Émile Durkheim (1858–1917), along with Marx and Weber, is considered one of the 'founding fathers' of modern sociology. In *The Rules of Sociological Method* he attempts to establish sociology as a positivistic science, insisting that it should have a specific object of study, and a recognised scientific method of objectivity. As such, he contrasted it with philosophy.

17   Marcel Mauss (1872–1950) was, in fact, Durkheim's nephew. He similarly worked in the area of sociology, but more with an anthropological bent. He became known for his theories around magic, sacrifice and gift exchange.

18   'Economy and Society'.

19   A seminal paper on this is Bourdieu 1971b/1966 'Intellectual field and creative project', where he articulates the importance of *champ*—or *field*—for the first time. See also Grenfell 2014a (chapter 4, and pp 221–24).

20 This work exists in various publications; a good summing up is in Bourdieu 1990a/1980 *The logic of practice* (Book 2, Part 3).

21 For a discussion of the derivation and significance of various forms of capital—*economic capital, social capital, cultural capital*—see Grenfell 2014a (chapters 6 and 13).

22 The *Collège de France* was founded in 1530, and brings together the most celebrated academics in France. There are just 50 or so in number and they are elected among themselves. Bourdieu was nominated Chair of Sociology there in 1980.

23 'Banal' in French really means 'trivial' or 'commonplace'. By using the word '*débanalisation*' Bourdieu intends to show how something that may seem ordinary or even mundane is actually quite significant.

24 The key works here are again: *An outline of a theory of practice* and *The logic of practice*.

25 Key texts here are: Bourdieu 1977b *Outline of a theory of practice* 171–83; and Bourdieu 1991a (Part III, chapter 7).

26 One of Bourdieu's first *fieldwork* studies was on the matrimonial strategies of the farmer communities in his home region of the Béarn, France. Three seminal papers arose from this work in 1962, 1972 and 1989. These are grouped together with a new introduction in Bourdieu 2008/2002, *The bachelors' ball*.

27 See Bourdieu (with Wacquant) 1989. Also Grenfell 2014a: 219ff.

28 Bourdieu 1996a/1989 *The state nobility. Elite schools in the field of power*.

29 The *École Polytechnique*—nicknamed the 'X'—is again one of the leading French *Grandes Écoles* set up in 1794. Its special focus is engineering, but really it attracts students aiming for the very highest level of French governance.

30 L'ENA stands for the *École Normale d'Administration*, another of the French *Grandes Écoles*; this one established in 1945 in order to train a new cadre of highly educated civil servants.

31 Bourdieu was a keen photographer. Indeed, many of his studies seem to arise from a single image (see Grenfell, 2006 for discussion). A sample of the photos he took in Algeria can be found in Bourdieu (2012/2003), *Picturing Algeria*. See also Endnote 4. A further discussion of Bourdieu and photography can be found in Hardy and Grenfell (2010)

32 See Grenfell 2014a (chapter 3).

33 See Grenfell 2004a (chapter 5); also Bourdieu 2014/1974.

34 The distinction between *rule* and *strategy* is fundamental to Bourdieu. See Endnote 33, and Grenfell 2014b. Similarly, he would be against *Rational Action Theory*, which seeks to model human behavior in terms of predictable rational choices.

35 Bourdieu 1991a/1982. Also Grenfell 2011, *Bourdieu, language and linguistics*.

36 Contemporary linguistics was founded by the Swiss academic Saussure (1857–1913), who set out a theoretical taxonomy for describing human languages: *langue, parole, signifier/signified*, which in turn was taken forward by structural linguists who sought to analyse the formal properties of language. Noam Chomsky (1928–) took this forward again from the 1950s, making a similar distinction between *Competence and Performance*, with a primary focus on the former—in particular, the *deep grammatical* structures which all languages shared. Bourdieu quite liked this distinction, which he saw as analogous to the way deep generative structures underpin diverse cultural practices. However, he was critical of the

attitude that attempted to find the meaning of language *in* language itself. In fact, the Chomskian paradigm has dominated contemporary linguistics since its inception, and those interested in the social derivation of language and the effect of local context have struggled somewhat to find a comparative theory and method. William Labov (1927–) is one such pioneering American sociolinguist, who has worked on the way language varies according to social origins and local application. See Bourdieu and Labov 1983. Bourdieu here refers to his earlier work, which set itself between Weinrich and Martinet. André Martinet (1908–1999) was a French structural linguist, but with a special interest in the functional aspects of syntax—which incidentally he opposed to Chomskian transformational grammar. Harald Weinrich (1927–) is a German linguist who specialised in tense, juxtaposing *narrative* and *commentary* (*récit* and *commentaire*). In the former, the attitude is descriptive, while in the latter the speaker takes on a 'point of view'. Thus the neutrality of language is set against its expression of social position. Weinrich relates this to the way specific tenses—past, present, future—are employed, and thus brings the social dimensions of language into a formal structural account. In a sense, this is what Bourdieu was attempting to do, both in his language studies and in his socio-cultural work more generally; i.e. integrating social variation within a formally descriptive account. See Grenfell 2011.

37 Bourdieu 1984/1979: 468.

38 Besides Flaubert's writings (see Endnote 42), one of Bourdieu's favourite books is *To the Lighthouse* by Virginia Woolf. He sees reproduced in this novel the whole social structure of which the protagonists are a part; how it is expressed in their very language and every gesture: the domination of the male patriarch—indeed, how he is dominated by his domination, by his unseeing relationship to the *illusio*—the interests of 'the game'. At

the same time, Bourdieu argues that Woolf allows us to see how a certain class of women of the day is able to avoid engaging with the *illusio*, and avoid the central games of society, and thus escape the *libido dominandi* that comes with such involvement. As a result, women develop a lucid view of what is going on—almost a sociological 'knowing' gaze (see Bourdieu, with Wacquant, 1992a: 173). In the world, and thus represented in the novel, everything is symbolic for Bourdieu. So, when the heroine Mrs Ramsay tries on a stocking, a whole set of events are triggered that can only be understood in terms of her social position and *habitus* (ibid: 124). In these ways, Woolf is using literary techniques—'fade in/fade out', for example—to express the 'mystic boundaries' between masculine and feminine worlds and the 'enchantment of love' (Bourdieu 2001/1998: 108): *Masculine domination*—the disillusioning in which she takes so much pleasure in bringing about (indeed, something that is shared with the sociologist!).

39 This was the academic review founded by Bourdieu in 1975: https://www.arss.fr/

40 The 'events' of 1968 culminated in a series of increasingly violent demonstrations in France—especially in Paris—between the 'forces of order' and students and striking workers. Not quite a revolution, it is nonetheless seen as a major crisis stemming from the rapid economic expansion which had occurred in France since the 5th Republic was formed in 1958. Ultimately, what happened ended the reign of President Charles De Gaulle, and led to a series of reforms across French society, although many of these are now seen as not having delivered what was promised.

41 Bourdieu 1988/1984, *Homo academicus*. This book is Bourdieu's study and analysis of the French academic field.

42 Gustave Flaubert (1821–1880) was a French novelist, and renown as an exponent of literary realism. His novels

are therefore seen as accounts of the times. His work period corresponded to revolutionary changes in French society that gave birth a new attitude of 'art for art's sake' among artists: for example, the Impressionists. Bourdieu's work on this is set out in Bourdieu 1996b/1992, *The Rules of Art*. Also, Bourdieu 2017/2013, *Manet: A symbolic revolution*. For further discussion of Bourdieu and art, see: Bourdieu 2016/1999 *Thinking about art at art school*, Canberra: Centre for Creative and Cultural Research; Grenfell and Hardy 2007, *Art rules: Bourdieu and the visual arts*; Grenfell 2004 (chapter 3).

43 Bourdieu was struck by the way history repeats itself, although often in a disguised way; this idea itself somewhat originating in Marx's declaration that when history repeats itself, the 'first time is tragedy and the second time is farce'. The *state nobility* (See Endnote 28) is predicated on this idea: it was published in the same year as the two hundredth anniversary of the Great French Revolution of 1789, implicitly suggesting that if the monarch had been disposed, a new 'State nobility' had replaced them as a 'noble elite'. The Revolution of 1848—often known as the 'February Revolution'—took place against a backdrop of protests and demonstrations across Europe, as did 1968. Moreover, again perhaps as 1968, it was essentially a 'conservative revolution': in 1848, and despite concessions, the events led, in effect, to the re-establishment of the monarchy through the crowning of Louis Bonaparte as head of the second French Empire; in 1968 various concessions were made, but State control intensified.

44 Bourdieu 1994a/1987, *In other words: Essays towards a reflexive sociology*.

45 Bourdieu 1992b 'Principles for reflecting on the curriculum', *The curriculum journal* 1.3: 307–14; originally published 1989 *Principes pour une réflexion sur les contenus d'enseignment*, a report originated from the Commission

chaired by Bourdieu and François Gros, *Ministère de l'Éducation nationale de la jeunesse et des sports*, March 1989. See Bourdieu 2008, in Poupeau and Discepolo (eds), *Political interventions: Social science and political action* (trans D Fernbach), Oxford: Polity Press; originally published 2002 *Interventions: 1961–2001 Science sociale et action politique*, Marseille: Agone.

46 The CFDT (French Democratic Confederation of Labour) is a trade union in France, formed in 1962 from various Christian worker groups.

47 See Bourdieu 1998/1996, *On television and journalism*.

48 Bourdieu (with Passeron and De Saint Martin) 1994b *Academic discourse*. Oxford: Polity; originally published 1965 *Rapport pédagogique et communication*, The Hague: Mouton

49 This is a research approach to studying the way people construct order in their daily lives, often in micro contexts. It is ethnographic in orientation but quite positivist in its attempts to tease out underlying rules of social exchange; for example, in discourse analysis.

50 See Endnotes 28 and 43.

51 Eternal recurrence of reflexivity: a reflection on a reflection on a reflection on a reflection ... etc—where nothing, finally, can be stable long enough to become manifest. See Grenfell and Pahl 2019 (chapter 9).

52 This occurred in the twentieth century when philosophers began to use the ideas of the Swiss linguist Ferdinand de Saussure (1857–1913): in particular, his 'discovery' that the relationship between a thing and the word that represented it—signified and signifier—was arbitrary. From this understanding, it is a short step to seeing all meaning as somehow arbitrary and contingent.

53 E. P. Thompson, see Bourdieu 1990b, 49.

54 The leading French exponents of so-called post-modernism/poststructuralism.

55 See Bourdieu 2003, 'Participant objectivation', *Journal of the Royal Anthropological Institute* 9.1: 28–42. Originally 'Participant objectivation—How to do it', address given in receipt of the Aldous Huxley Medal for Anthropology, University of London, 12 November, 2000, *Mimeograph*, 12pp. Also Bourdieu 2004/2001, *Science of science and reflexivity*. Cambridge: Part III Ch. 1; Grenfell 2014a: 224ff; and Grenfell and Pahl 2019 (chapter 9).

56 Bronislaw Kasper Malinowski (1884–1942) was a Polish-born British anthropologist of some renown, specialising in studies of Australian Aboriginals and other indigenous people in the Pacific area.

57 See Endnote 7. Also Bourdieu (with Chamboredon and Passeron) 1991b/1968, *The craft of sociology.*

58 Richard Rorty (1931–2007) was an American philosopher who, in one of his most well-known books—*Philosophy and the mirror of nature*—argued for a pragmatic approach to philosophy; he hence was critical of the postmodern turn it had taken, as much as those who would see philosophy as a 'mirror of reality'.

59 Husserl was a colleague of Martin Heidegger (1889–1976) who took the phenomenological account of philosophy a stage further into interpretative hermeneutics and existentialism. He is the key figure in modern existentialism and heavily influenced Sartre (see Endnote 7). Bourdieu's own account of Heidegger and the way his work (and its links with fascism) can be understood against an analysis of the philosophical field in Germany in the early parts of the twentieth century is among his best work; see Bourdieu 1991c/1988. See Endnote 8.

60 Alfred Schütz (1899–1958) was an Austrian philosopher who very much built on the work of Husserl, especially in relating it to the social sciences.

61   See Grenfell 2014a (chapter 7).

62   Karl Marx (1818–1883) was a highly influential thinker, philosopher, economist, historian and polemicist. He is attributed with having founded modern communism, but was equally influential in the development of socialist ideas; he is also considered one of the 'founding fathers'— along with Emile Durkheim (1858–1917) and Max Weber (1864–1920)—of sociology. Marx was very interested in Hegel's philosophy; in particular, the notion of the dialectic—that things proceeded through a dynamic of thesis -> antithesis -> synthesis. But, whereas Hegel interpreted this relationship in terms of ideas and human spirit, Marx saw it in terms of *dialectical materialism*: the primacy of matter—in this case *capital*—over ideas. This distinction itself unleashed one of the seminal arguments in both philosophy and sociology: the question of the salience of ideas or the objective environment in the development of human discourse. In one sense, of course, it is a non-argument, and both ideas and environment constitute what happens—or not. Weber's own *Protestant Ethic and the Spirit of Capitalism* (1904/1905) takes this line as a kind of complement, or corrective, to Marx's thesis, rather than direct opposition to it (see Endnote 12). However, it is arguable that Marx also appreciated such an argument. Later in life, and under the influence of Friedrich Engels (1820–1895), Marx's political mission became more acute, and with it his espousal of 'dialectical materialism' and political activism. However, there is much evidence that the young Marx fully appreciated the importance of ideas and sensations in forming the content of human thought and action. Indeed, in his 1844 'Theses on Feuerbach' (a German philosopher who mounted a 'materialist'—i.e. human—critique of religion) Marx writes: 'The principal defect of all materialism up to now—including that of Feuerbach—is that the external object, reality, the sensible world, is grasped in the form

of *an object or an intuition*; but not as *concrete human activity*, as *practice*, in a subjective way. That is why the active aspect was developed in idealism, in opposition to materialism—but *only* in an abstract way, since idealism naturally does not know real concrete activity as such'. The fact that Bourdieu uses this quote as an epigraph to his major text on his theory of practice (the *Outline*), indicates how important he saw it to understand the link between the material and ideal—object and subject—in relational (structural) terms. See Bourdieu 1977b: vi; and also Bourdieu 1990a/1980: 25ff.

63 I retain 'reflexion' in the French to draw attention to the fact that it is not quite the same as the English 'reflection'. Bourdieu is here talking about the issue of a 'subject that does not make of itself an object'. See Grenfell and Pahl 2019 (chapter 9).

64 This position would be very close to that of the Austrian philosopher Karl Popper (1902–1994), who argued that a 'critical community' is essential in any scientific *field* in order to verify truth claims. Bourdieu argues that science is more objective the more such a community is autonomous, since in this case they are uninfluenced, if reflexive, by outside pressures. However, Bourdieu would not accept Popper's notion of truth as 'objective knowledge without a knowing subject'; that is, independent of human though (see Bourdieu 1984/1979: 228). But the argument goes beyond this issue and seems to suggest that the 'empirical subject' is more themselves the more they are collective in such terms; that is, constituted by human rather than societal forces. In this way, sociology for Bourdieu offers a means towards a new form of humanism, 'torn' away from the pernicious influences of society but reconstituted in a new enlightened form, which itself arises from what is available collectively (socially). His sociology is the way to achieve this position; see Bourdieu 2003 and; Grenfell 2004 (chapter 7).

References

I always insist that readers of Bourdieu pay attention to the exact time period when various publications appeared since they were often produced in response to specific events, both socio-politically and intellectually. This is to encourage what Bourdieu referred to as a 'socio-genetic' reading of his work. At the same time, I am aware that for the majority of readers of this text, English will be their main working medium. In listing the various references associated with these interviews, therefore, I set the English version of particular writings first, followed by the original French. Occasionally, there are no equivalents. The first date given refers to the English version and the second date the French. For a comprehensive list of all of Bourdieu's output, I would recommend Deslaut, Y and Rivière, M-C 2002 Bibliographie des travaux de Pierre Bourdieu: suivi d'un entretien sur l'esprit de la recherche, *Pantin: Le Temps des Cerises.*

Bourdieu, P 1958 *Sociologie de l'Algérie* (revised and corrected edition, 1961), Paris: Que Sais-je

Bourdieu, P 1961 'Révolution dans la révolution', *Esprit* (Jan): 27–40

Bourdieu, P 1962a *The Algerians* (trans ACM Ross), Boston: Beacon Press

Bourdieu, P 1962b 'De la guerre révolutionnaire à la révolution', in F Perroux (ed), *L'Algérie de demain*, Paris: PUF, 5–13

Bourdieu, P, with A Darbel, JP Rivet, and C Seibel 1963 *Travail et travailleurs en Algérie*, Paris, The Hague: Mouton

Bourdieu, P, with A Sayad 1964a *Le déracinement, la crise de l'agriculture tradionelle en Algérie*, Paris: Les Editions de Minuit

Bourdieu, P, with J-C Passeron 1964b *Les étudiants et leurs études*, Paris, The Hague, Mouton: Cahiers du Centre de Sociologie Européenne

Bourdieu, P 1971a 'Systems of education and systems of thought', in MFD Young (ed) *Knowledge and control: New directions for the sociology of education*, London: Macmillan, 189–207; originally published 1967 'Systèmes d'enseignement et systèmes de pensée', *Revue internationale des sciences sociales* XIX.3: 338–88

Bourdieu, P 1971b 'Intellectual field and creative project', in MFD Young (ed) *Knowledge and control: New directions for the sociology of education*, London: Macmillan, 161–88; originally published 1966 'Champ intellectuel et projet créateur', *Les Temps Modernes* (Nov): 865–906

Bourdieu, P, with J-C Passeron 1977a *Reproduction in education, society and culture* (trans R Nice), London: Sage; originally published 1970 *La reproduction. Eléments pour une théorie du système d'enseignement*, Paris: Editions de Minuit

Bourdieu, P 1977b *Outline of a theory of practice* (trans R Nice), Cambridge: Cambridge University

Press; originally published 1972 *Esquisse d'une théorie de la pratique. Précédé de trois études d'ethnologie Kabyle*, Geneva: Droz

Bourdieu, P & J-C Passeron 1979 *The inheritors: French students and their relation to culture* (trans R Nice), Chicago: The University of Chicago Press; originally published 1964 *Les héritiers, les étudiants et la culture*, Paris: Les Editions de Minuit

Bourdieu, P and W Labov 1983 'Le changement linguistique: entretien avec William Labov', *Actes de la recherche en sciences sociales* 46: 67–72

Bourdieu, P 1984 *Distinction: A social critique of the judgement of taste* (trans R Nice), Oxford: Polity; originally published 1979 *La Distinction. Critique sociale du jugement*, Paris: Editions de Minuit

Bourdieu, P 1988 *Homo academicus* (trans P Collier), Oxford: Polity; originally published 1984 *Homo academicus*, Paris: Les Editions de Minuit

Bourdieu, P, with L Wacquant 1989 'Towards a reflexive sociology: A workshop with Pierre Bourdieu', *Sociological theory* 7.1: 26–63

Bourdieu, P 1990a *The logic of practice* (trans R Nice), Oxford: Polity; originally published 1980 *Le sens pratique*, Paris: Les Editions de Minuit

Bourdieu, P 1990b *In Other words: Essays towards a Reflexive Sociology* (trans M Adamson). Oxford: Polity; original published in 1987 *Choses dites*. Paris: Editions de Minuit

Bourdieu, P 1991a *Language and symbolic power* (trans G Raymond and M Adamson), Oxford: Polity Press; originally published 1982 *Ce que parler veut dire*, Paris: Fayard

Bourdieu, P, with J-C Chamboredon and J-C Passeron 1991b *The craft of sociology* (trans R Nice), New York: Walter de Gruyter; originally published 1968 *Le métier de sociologue*, Paris: Mouton-Bordas

Bourdieu, P 1991c *The political ontology of Martin Heidegger* (trans P Collier), Oxford: Polity Press; originally published 1988 *L'ontologie politique de Martin Heidegger*, Paris: Les Éditions de Minuit

Bourdieu, P, with L Wacquant 1992a *An invitation to reflexive sociology*, Oxford: Polity Press; originally published 1992 *Réponses: Pour une anthropologie reflexive*, Paris: Seuil

Bourdieu, P 1992b 'Principles for reflecting on the curriculum', *The curriculum journal* 1.3: 307–14; originally published 1989 'Principes pour une réflexion sur les contenus d'enseignment', *Ministère de l'Éducation nationale de la jeunesse et des sports*, March 1989; see also P Bourdieu (ed. F Poupeau and T Discepolo) 2002 *Interventions: 1961–2001 Science sociale et action politique*, Marseille: Agone (pp. 217–226); and 'Principles for a discussion of the contents of education', in P Bourdieu 2008 *Political interventions: Social science and political action* (ed. F Poupeau and T Discepolo, trans D Fernbach), Oxford: Polity Press, 173–80

Bourdieu, P 1994a *In other words: Essays towards a reflexive sociology* (trans M Adamson), Oxford: Polity; originally published 1987 *Choses dites*, Paris: Les Editions de Minuit

Bourdieu, P, with J-C Passeron and M De Saint Martin 1994b *Academic discourse*. Oxford: Polity; originally published 1965 *Rapport pédagogique et communication*, The Hague: Mouton

Bourdieu, P 1996a *The state nobility. Elite schools in the field of power* (trans LC Clough), Oxford: Polity Press; originally published 1989 *La noblesse d'état. Grandes écoles et esprit de corps*, Paris: Les Editions de Minuit

Bourdieu, P 1996b *The rules of art* (trans S Emanuel), Oxford: Polity Press; originally published 1992 *Les règles de l'art. Genèse et structure du champ litéraire*, Paris: Seuil

Bourdieu, P 1998 *On television and journalism*, London: Pluto Press; originally published 1996 *Sur la télévision, suivi de l'emprise du journalisme*, Paris: Raisons d'agir

Bourdieu, P 2001 *Masculine domination*, Oxford: Polity Press; originally published 1998 *La domination masculine*, Paris: Seuil

Bourdieu, P 2002 'Pierre par Bourdieu—Le Rosebud de Pierre Bourdieu', *Le Nouvel Observateur*, Paris (31 Jan): 30–31

Bourdieu, P 2003 'Participant objectivation', *Journal of the Royal Anthropological Institute* 9.1: 28–42

Bourdieu, P 2004 *Science of science and reflexivity* (trans R Nice), Cambridge: Polity Press; originally published 2001 *Science de la science et réflexivité*, Paris: Raisons d'Agir

Bourdieu, P 2007 *Sketch for a self-analysis*, Cambridge: Cambridge University Press; originally published 2004 *Esquisse pour une auto-analyse*, Paris: Raisons d'Agir

Bourdieu, P 2008 *The bachelors' ball*, Oxford: Polity Press; originally published 2002 *Le bal des célibataires. Crise de la société en Béarn*, Paris: Seuil

Bourdieu, P 2012 *Picturing Algeria*, Columbia University Press; originally published 2003 *Images d'Algérie*, Paris: Actes Sud

Bourdieu, P 2014 'The future of class and the causality of the probable' (trans M Grenfell), in A Christoforou and M Lainé (eds), *Re-thinking economics: Exploring the work of Pierre Bourdieu*, London: Routledge, 233–69; originally published 1974 'Avenir de classe et causalité du probable', *Revue française de la sociologie* 15.1: 3–42

Bourdieu, P 2016 *Thinking about art at art school* (trans M Grenfell), Canberra: Centre for Creative and Cultural Research, University of Canberra; 1999 *Penser l'art à l'école*, University of Nîmes

Bourdieu, P 2017 *Manet: A symbolic revolution*, London: Polity Press; originally published 2013 *Manet: Une révolution symbolique*, Paris: Seuil

Durkheim, E 1982 *The rules of sociological method* (trans WD Halls), New York: Free Press; originally published 1894 *Les Règles de la Méthode Sociologique*, Paris: Payot

Eakin, E 2001 'Social status tends to seal one's fate', *New York Times*, 6 January

Grenfell, M 2004 *Pierre Bourdieu: Agent provocateur*, London: Continuum

Grenfell, M 2006 'Bourdieu in the field: from the Béarn to Algeria—a timely response', *French cultural studies* 17.2: 223–40

Grenfell, M 2007 *Bourdieu, education and training*, London: Continuum

Grenfell, M 2011 *Bourdieu, language and linguistics*, London: Continuum

Grenfell, M 2012 (with B Street, J Rowsell, K Pahl, D Bloome, C Hardy) *Language, ethnography and education: Bourdieu and new literacy studies.* London: Routledge

Grenfell, M (ed) 2014a *Pierre Bourdieu: Key concepts* (2nd ed), London: Routledge

Grenfell, M 2014b 'Capital conversions in post-modern economies', in A Christoforou and M Lainé (eds), *Re-thinking economics: Exploring the work of Pierre Bourdieu*, London: Routledge, 143–60

Grenfell, M 2014c *Pierre Bourdieu: Bloomsbury Library of Educational Thought*, London: Bloomsbury

Grenfell, M and C Hardy 2007 *Art rules: Bourdieu and the visual arts*, Oxford: Berg

Grenfell, M and F Lebaron (eds) 2014 *Bourdieu and data analysis*, Berne: Lang

Grenfell, M and K Pahl 2019 *Bourdieu, language-based ethnography and reflexivity: Putting theory into practice*, New York: Routledge

Hardy, C and Grenfell, M (2010) 'Snaps! Bourdieu and the Field of Photographic Art', *International Journal of Arts in Society* 5, 1: 49-62

Loubet del Bayle, J-L 1969 *Les non-conformistes des années* 30, Paris: Seuil

Marx, K 'Theses on Feuerbach' 1970 in *The German Ideology* (with Friedrich Engels), New York: International Publishers, 121–23; originally written 1845, originally published 1888 in F Engels, Ludwig *Feuerbach und der Ausgang der Klassischen deutschen Philosophie ... Mit Anhang Karl Marx über Feuerbach von Jahre* 1845, Berlin: Verlag von JHW Dietz, 69–72

Weber, M 1958 *Protestant Ethic and the Spirit of Capitalism* (trans T Parsons), New York: Scribner

Acknowledgements

My heart-felt thanks must firstly go to Pierre Bourdieu (1930–2002) for the support and friendship he extended to me over the time we worked together. Specifically, for this project, I am grateful for his openness in allowing himself to be interviewed by me on various occasions. More than this, however, he also shared with me the job of editing the transcripts of our conversations; an experience that enabled me to see in action what he calls in these interviews, 'the relationship between the *empirical habitus* and the *scientific habitus*'. Parts of these texts were originally published in French as Occasional Paper 37 of the Centre for Language in Education at the University of Southampton, UK. This current translated version is extended and annotated.

I also express my profound thanks to Distinguished Professor Jen Webb, Director of the Centre for Creative and Cultural Research in the Faculty of Arts and Design at the University of Canberra, Australia. She has been an enthusiastic and supportive colleague, and in ways too numerous to list here. More specifically, she read the text on repeated occasions with a scrupulous attention to detail. I thank her for suggestions, which enlarged the scope of the original piece, and many other points, which improved both its form and content. Her team, especially Shane Strange and Caren Florance, have undertaken a range of editing and graphic tasks, which have turned my original copy into the attractive publication it now is. I also thank Fabio Ribeiro for detailed feedback.

Thanks to all these.

Lightning Source UK Ltd.
Milton Keynes UK
UKHW020613180220
358905UK00012B/1106

9 780648 553724